The STRANGE *and* CURIOUS GUIDE *to* TRAUMA

The Strange and Curious Guide to Trauma

Sally Donovan

Illustrated by Emmi Smid

Jessica Kingsley Publishers

London and Philadelphia

First published in Great Britain in 2022 by Jessica Kingsley Publishers
An imprint of Hodder & Stoughton
An Hachette Company

1

Front cover design by Emmi Smid.

A CIP catalogue record for this title is available from the British Library and the Library of Congress

ISBN 978 1 78775 747 9
eISBN 978 1 78775 748 6

Printed and bound in Great Britain by TJ Books Limited

Jessica Kingsley Publishers' policy is to use papers that are natural, renewable and recyclable products and made from wood grown in sustainable forests. The logging and manufacturing processes are expected to conform to the environmental regulations of the country of origin.

Jessica Kingsley Publishers
Carmelite House
50 Victoria Embankment
London EC4Y 0DZ

www.jkp.com

Contents

List of Characters

Barry:
A bin lorry driver.

Morris and Robyn:
Wheelie bin emptier outers.

Percy: A most perfect carrot (at least that's what he thinks).

Wendy: A wonky and interesting carrot.

Amy: Amy Amygdala is an almond-shaped piece of brain deep inside our nut heads. She scans our surroundings for danger.

Courtney: Courtney Cortisol is a chemical that travels in our blood. She gives us extra focus and energy to escape from danger.

Adrian: Adrian Adrenaline is a chemical that travels in our blood. He gives our bodies superpowers of escape.

Some People: They look and sound like ordinary people but they are behind with the science and believe Wrong Things.

Tony: A baboon who enjoys hanging about in trees. Also the owner of The Big Baboon, a café and disco.

Ordinary Jo: That's me.

1

Baboon Tuesday 1: An Ordinary Day

Baboon Tuesday began much like any other ordinary Tuesday.

I woke up in an ordinary way, got out of my ordinary bed, put on my ordinary clothes, cleaned my ordinary teeth and put on my ordinary coat.

It was Bin Lorry Day, which is how I know it was a Tuesday.

I like Bin Lorry Day. It is the highlight of my ordinary week.

On Bin Lorry Day, I sit on the wall outside our house and wait for the bin lorry to drive into our ordinary road. I wave to Barry, the bin lorry driver, and he waves back. Then I nod to Robyn and Morris as they wheel my neighbours' bins to the back of the lorry and attach them to the mechanism that swings the bins high into the air.

'Morning, Robyn. Morning, Morris,' I say.

'Morning, Ordinary Jo,' they reply.

I point to my bin and say, 'Here's my bin,' and they reply, 'Nice one, mate.'

This is exactly what happens every Tuesday. It's exactly what happened the day that turned out to be Baboon Tuesday.

My name is Ordinary Jo and I'm getting ahead of myself. This is a book about trauma, not a book about bin lorries. Trauma isn't ordinary. But it can happen to anyone.

Even ordinary people like me.

2

To Bees or Not to Bees: Trauma

Trauma is a word that means an injury to the body, like a purple bruise or a broken bone.

It also means an injury to a person's inside life – their thoughts and feelings. These are still hurts even though they are invisible.

These are the kinds of hurts *The Strange and Curious Guide to Trauma* is about – injuries to our inside lives.

Trauma is caused by experiences that are so bad and so scary that our bodies decide we could be in the deepest danger.

Trauma can be difficult to read and talk about. It can bring on strange feelings in the tummy area, or the head area, or the leg areas, or the anywhere really areas. The strange feelings can get trapped in our bodies and buzz around the place like a bee in a shoebox. A swarm of bees in a shoebox even.

If this happens to you while you read this book, it's fine to step outside and smell the flowers, shake your body, stamp your feet and stretch out your arms as wide as they can reach.

It's also fine to stroke a kitten* or crunch an ice cube or blow a giant bubble. Work that body. BUZZZ.

Trauma is an invisible hurt and an epic story of survival.

Our book about trauma features buzzy bees stuck in your tummy, yes, and also science and superheroes, carrots and lambs, lollies and, unfortunately for me, baboons.

Well, one baboon in particular, but I'm not ready to introduce him quite yet.

*with the written permission of the kitten.

3

Where Trauma Comes From: A Tale of Two Carrots

There are many different experiences that can cause trauma, such as being seriously ill, being separated from the people you love, or being hurt or rejected by the people who should look after you.

Other examples are being bullied or threatened, living in a time and place of war, not having enough food to eat, or being in a scary car accident. These are awful things to happen to anyone.

Trauma is

OVERWHELMING FEAR

Trauma is

DANGER IS REALLY, REALLY NEAR

Trauma is

GET ME OUT OF HERE

You get the idea.

Facts about Trauma

It's important to know about trauma because it can affect absolutely anyone. Knowing about trauma helps us to understand:

- It is not a person's fault if they have experienced trauma.
- It is not a person's fault if it is difficult for them to recover from trauma.
- It is not a person's fault if they have ways of coping with trauma.
- Coping with trauma is a strength and a superpower.

It looks like there's a theme here.

A Tale of Two Carrots

Carrot Percy is a perfect carrot.

He is so perfect he is in the Perfect Vegetables section of the supermarket. Percy is long and

smooth and chunky. He is pleased with himself for being such a gorgeous hunk of a carrot.

He was once on the front cover of *Carrot World* – a magazine for good-looking carrots and other root vegetables.

Carrot Wendy is a wonky carrot. She is to be found on the Wonky Shelf in the supermarket with all the other less than perfect-looking vegetables. Wendy is knobbly and lumpy and has two sort of carroty legs.

She has never been on the front cover of *Carrot World*.

We could compare Carrot Percy and Carrot Wendy. We could admire Percy for his longness and smoothness. We could look down on Wendy for her knobbly-bobblyness and wonder why she didn't try harder to grow straight and smooth like Percy.

But before we get all judgey, let's first take a look at where Perfect Percy and Wonky Wendy grew up.

Percy grew in the most perfect soil a carrot could wish for – if carrots had wishes, which they don't. It was fine and deep and full of all the nutrients. Lucky Percy!

Wendy grew in soil that was not ideal for carrots because it was stony. Stones are obstacles to a growing carrot. But did Wendy give up and stop growing every time her little carroty root touched a stone? No, she did not.

Wendy, like all living things, is a determined SURVIVOR.

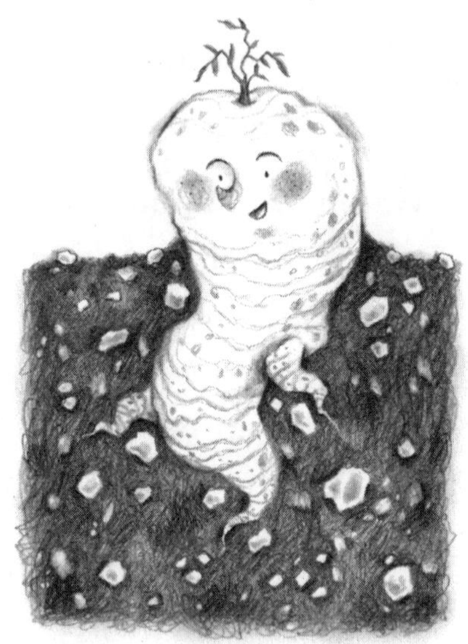

She grew around the stones and in different directions wherever she could. This means she looks a bit different from carrots like Percy. But she tastes just as good and she is an interesting and curious shape.

If she took a picture of herself and sent it to interestingcarrots.com, she could win over £50.

It's not fair, or scientifically correct, to blame carrots, or indeed any plant, for the soil they grew up in.

Was it Wendy's fault that she grew in soil that happened to have stones in? No, it was not. Here, in *The Strange and Curious Guide to Trauma*, we don't blame carrots. We accept all carrots just as they are.

And that's because we are about facts and knowledge and one other thing.

That one other thing is *kindness*.

Knowledge about Trauma

Having knowledge about trauma can help us to understand other people and ourselves better.

It can help us to understand how incredible life on Earth is and how awesome we all are. It might even help everyone to be a bit kinder to each other and themselves.

This is why knowing about trauma is a superpower.

4

The Drive to Stay Alive

All living things have the same aim: to stay alive and make more of themselves. Carrots. Worms. Bacteria. Baboons. Even humans.

They are all busy surviving and reproducing.

Humans exist to stay alive and make more humans. It's pretty basic, but that's the science.

There's a lot more to having a good and interesting life than staying alive and having babies, obvs.

Like, for example, sitting on a wall, watching a wheelie bin being attached to the back of a bin lorry and swung high, high into the sky. You get the idea.

When we are in danger of not surviving, our bodies do everything in their power to keep us alive and safe. Our bodies are extremely good at this. They're looking after our safeness and aliveness every second of every day, which is pretty clever of them.

5

DANGERS! Different Kinds of Dangers to Our Aliveness

Ordinary Dangers to Our Aliveness

Ordinary dangers to our aliveness are everyday things like getting too cold, being too thirsty, or not having enough energy to get out of bed in time to see the bin lorry.

Our bodies are so expert at managing these ordinary dangers that we don't know they are doing it most of the time.

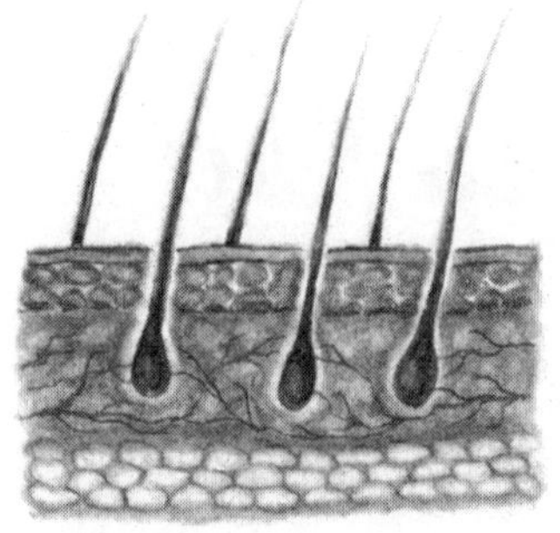

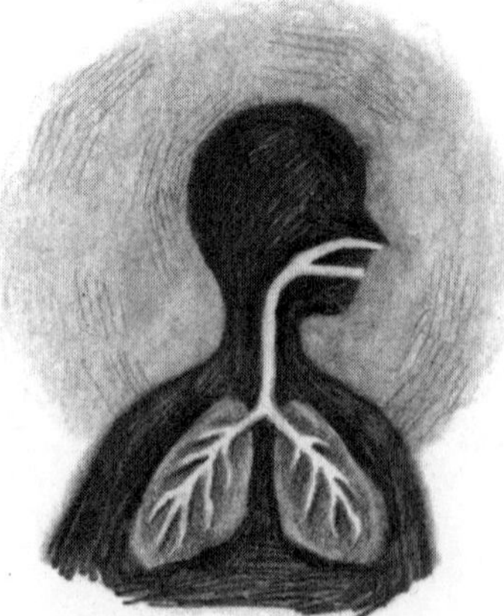

When we are chilly, our bodies shiver and make our hairs stand on end like an instant woolly jumper. They sweat when we are hot to cool us down. They make us want to drink and eat when we need to. They keep us breathing in and out all day long.

Our bodies do loads and loads of clever stuff like this. And it's automatic. We don't have to spend time thinking about it. Which is a good job. Wouldn't thinking about it all the time be hard work? It would also be very boring.

Our clever, strange and curious bodies are keeping us safe all the time. Perhaps they deserve more thanks than we give them.

Extra-Ordinary Dangers to Our Aliveness

Extra-ordinary dangers are not about feeling chilly or fancying a glass of water.

Extra-ordinary dangers are big surprises that come out of nowhere and scare us half out of our skins.

6

Baboon Tuesday 2: A Screech and a Swear

After I said goodbye to Barry, Robyn and Morris and watched the bin lorry disappear out of sight, I headed off to The Big Tree on top of The Big Hill.

The reason I headed off to The Big Tree on top of The Big Hill is because dangling from The Big Tree is a swing. Swinging on the swing that dangles from The Big Tree on The Big Hill is one of my favourite things to do.

It feels a bit like flying.

I sat on the swing and put my hand inside my coat pocket.

I was surprised to find a fizzy orange lolly there. It was a bit sticky and a little bit fluffy, but my mouth was watering even before I'd peeled the wrapper off. I can remember thinking, 'How strange that my mouth is watering even before I've got the wrapper off. What's *that* all about?'

I licked my lolly and watched my favourite funny video on my phone. The video is of lots of goats making ridiculous noises that sound like humans shouting.

'AAAAAHAAAAHAAAAA,' they shout, with their

goaty mouths open and their grotty, goaty tongues sticking right out.

'AAAAAAAAAHAAAA.'

'AAAAAAAAAHHAAAHHAAA.'

It was hilarious.

It was so hilarious I laughed out loud even though I was on my own on top of The Big Hill.

Or so I'd thought.

All of a sudden.

A rustling noise.

Or was it?

Up in the tree.

Very faint.

Barely a noise at all.

But there was definitely a something.

I froze.

My ears strained to hear the something.

Then...

CRRRRAAAAASSH!!!

BEHIND ME.

RIGHT. BEHIND. ME.

All at once I did a screech and a swear, jumped off the swing and threw my lolly and my phone to the ground.

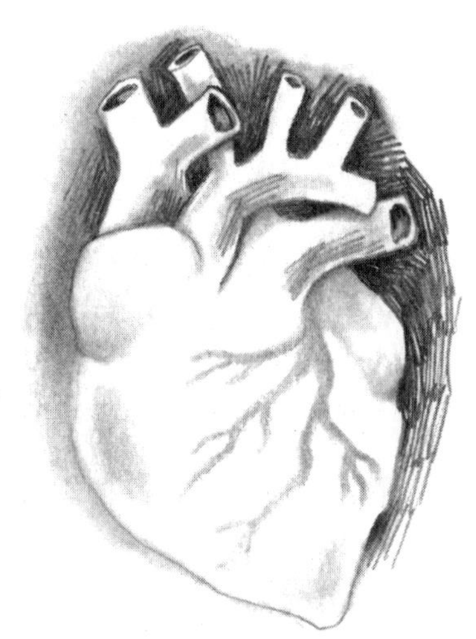

My heart was *beating* very, very fast and hard, like it was going to burst out of my chest and run away.

My stomach *flittered* and *flapped* as if a swarm of bees was buzzing around inside it.

My eyes opened *super-wide* and *round* like dinner plates.

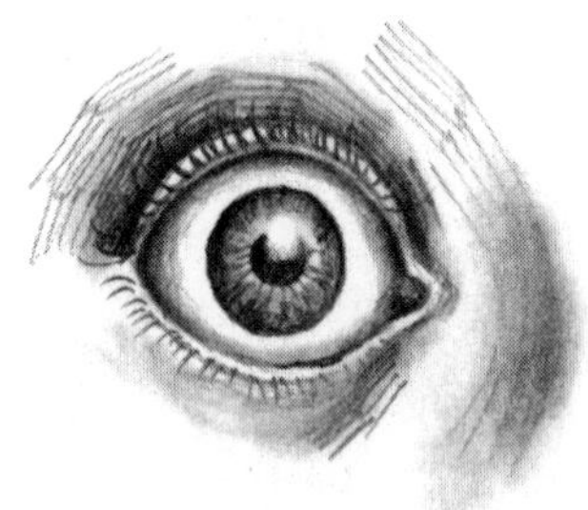

A low growl.

I held my breath.

And slowly, so slowly, I turned around to find out WHAT ON EARTH HAD JUST LANDED.

Can you guess what it was?

I'll give you a clue: it wasn't a goat.

It was a massive, huge, giant, enormous, hairy, growly, angry-looking BABABABOOOOOOON.

7

PAUSE! What Happened to Me on Baboon Tuesday?

Let's pause the story a moment and consider my dilemma.

That Tuesday, when a massive baboon jumped down from The Big Tree and scared me out of my skin, my body did loads of things I did not choose for it to do.

1. It froze still.
2. It did a screech and a swear.
3. It threw my lolly and my phone on the ground.

I didn't choose for my body to do any of these things, just like I didn't ask it to dribble at the thought of licking my fizzy orange lolly.

I'll tell you what else I didn't do.

I didn't call out for help, 'Excuse me, can anyone assist me? I appear to be in a situation here.'

I didn't say to myself, 'Hey, Ordinary Jo, let's take some time to think through this problem.'

Because guess what would have happened if I had done any of those things?

Correct, again. (You're good at this.)

I'd have found myself on the menu at The Big Baboon Café and Disco. I think we can agree that would not have been good for my aliveness.

No, this was not the time for the brainy part of my brain to get involved.

It might be quite good at adding numbers up and finding the verbs in a sentence, but it is NOT the dude you call on in an emergency. It is RUBBISH in an emergency.

Here's a question.

Question: If I, Ordinary Jo, wasn't in control of my body, what was?

Listen in. This is going to get stranger and curiouser.

8

Meet Amy, Adrian and Courtney

When that baboon jumped down from that tree, a life-saving part of my brain called the amygdala took control of my body. We'll call her Amy Amygdala. She won't mind.

Amy is a little almond-shaped piece of brain, deep inside our heads where the sun don't shine. She's specially designed for EMERGENCY SITUATIONS.

A baboon jumping out of a tree behind a person minding their own business is, I'm sure you'll agree, an EMERGENCY SITUATION.

A NUTTY THOUGHT

It is strange and rather curious that our amygdalas are almond-shaped. An almond is a nut, but I expect you already know that. Our brains are shaped a bit like a walnut and our skulls, which protect our precious brains, are sometimes called our nuts.

It's all very nutty in there. Very nutty indeed.

Amy Amygdala's job is to scan our surroundings for danger. She's a bit like a smoke detector or a lifeguard at a swimming pool.

She scans all day long without complaining. Most of the time we have no idea of the important job she is doing for us. Until, that is, DANGER drops out of a tree and scares us out of our skins.

Then she takes control of our bodies.

She's fast.

She's efficient.

She doesn't have time for fancy problem-solving.

Amy's job is to keep us ALIVE.

Once you know a bit about Amy Amygdala, you will notice her fine and fast work as you go about your day.

It is Amy who helps us to leap out of the way of a speeding car before we've even realized we've seen or heard a speeding car.

It is Amy who notices a faraway rumble of thunder.

It is Amy who spots a tiny spider running across the floor.

It is Amy who reacts before we've even noticed a speeding car, a rumble of faraway thunder or a tiny spider, which is very quick indeed.

She is one impressive, nut-shaped piece of brain kit.

Her impressiveness doesn't end there.

She has some powerful and energetic friends. They can't wait to meet you. I'll let them introduce themselves. You'll have to forgive them because they talk *very quickly*.

Are you ready?

Adrian Adrenaline

My name is Adrian Adrenaline but you can call me Adrian for short I am a chemical that travels in your blood and when Amy sends me an urgent message I get to work immediately I give your body what it needs to get away from danger and I make your heart beat faster and your muscles stronger and your lungs bigger and I open up your eyes so you can see better and your ears so you can hear better and, and, and...

Slow down, Adrian!

Hang on, who's this barging on to the page?

Courtney Cortisol

My name is Courtney Cortisol and I am also a chemical that travels in your blood and I give you EXTRA ENERGY. I STOP you doing anything that is not REALLY, REALLY ESSENTIAL to keep you SAFE and ALIVE. You know that little bit of wee that comes out when you're scared? You can thank me for that!

Me and Adrian, together, we give you MAX ENERGY and MAX FOCUS. We give you powers!

9

Baboon Tuesday 3: Run for My Life

So, Adrian Adrenaline and Courtney Cortisol are impressive and everything, but back to the story of Baboon Tuesday.

I was standing so close to a scary baboon that I could feel his hot breath on my face.

I could see his sharp teeth. I could smell his body spray. And I could tell from the way he furrowed his eyebrow that he was working out what he was going to do.

How were Adrian Adrenaline and Courtney Cortisol going to get me out of this sticky situation? How was I going to avoid ending up on the menu at The Big Baboon Café and Disco?

Basically, like any person, in any dangerous situation, I had three options.

1. I could FIGHT the baboon.

2. I could RUN from the baboon.

3. I could be really still and quiet, pretend to be a tree or something and kind of HIDE from the baboon.

FIGHT for my life, RUN for my life or HIDE for my life?

To be honest, I've had better days.

The baboon opened his mouth. It was a huge, dark mouth with two sharp teeth like tusks set into gums the colour of foam shrimps. I'm not ashamed to say that a bit of wee came out. Normally, I would care if a bit of wee came out. I did not care.

I was more worried about being made into a pizza and served up at The Big Baboon Café and Disco.

Then.

From down on the ground...

A muffled noise...

A kind of snorting...

Then AAAAAAHHHHHHHAAAAA!

The shouting goats!

A bit more wee came out.

The baboon looked puzzled, slowly bent down, picked up my phone and gazed at the screen. Then something else on the ground caught his eye. Something covered in dirt and leaves. He grunted, inspected it and poked it with his long, baboony fingers.

It was my fizzy orange lolly. He obviously had no idea what it was. It was a novelty to him, which was lucky for me. It gave me the chance to RRRUUUUUUUNNNN.

RUN FOR MY LIFE.

I don't remember deciding to run. I just did. My legs took off and I ran and ran and ran and ran and ran and ran and ran.

And then I ran a bit more.

Thanks to Adrian Adrenaline and Courtney Cortisol, I had the MAX ENERGY and MAX FOCUS to run faster than I had ever run in my life, ever. I was like a top athlete sprinting for a gold medal.

I ran down The Big Hill across the field and up the road back to my house.

10

Ladies and Gentlemen: Baby versus Lamb

Danger Danger!

Some scares and dangers happen once, like Baboon Tuesday.

Others take place over a long time, such as living somewhere unsafe, not being cared for, or being ill in hospital.

These kinds of dangers are scary and stressful a lot of the time. These kinds of dangers can shape how a person sees and experiences the world.

Living in danger can be kind of normal for some people. This is especially true when small children live in dangerous situations.

Sometimes we feel in danger even after the actual danger has passed. To understand why, let's look at some strange and curious facts about brains.

Human Brains

We humans believe ourselves to be *very clever*. We think we've got all the *skillz*.

We have invented computers and robots and medicines.

WALL OF CLEVER HUMANS

MARTIN LUTHER KING
-ACTIVIST-

NINA SIMONE
-MUSICIAN-

FRIDA KAHLO
-ARTIST-

ALBERT EINSTEIN
-PHYSICIST-

We have built cities with high-rise towers and underground trains and airports.

We have created art and music, and we use language and writing to say things to each other.

We are *top of the league of clever animals* (or so we like to think).

But what about our babies? You don't see too many of them inventing computers, building airports or painting pictures.

Most of them can't even put their own shoes on. It's curious. And rather strange.

Within hours of being born, a lamb can stand up, walk about and feed from its mother.

Within a couple of weeks, it can run, climb and mess around with its lamb friends in little lamb gangs.

At around four months old, it starts to become independent from its mother, has driving lessons and gets its first job.

Human babies by comparison are pretty helpless and vulnerable.

They don't usually stand up on their little chubby legs until they are around nine months old.

They don't usually walk until they are a year old. Even then, they are what could best be described as 'wobbly'.

Question: Why do lambs grow up so quickly and human babies so slowly?

Now there's a strange and curious question.

If lambs lay around on the ground gurgling and crying, they would get eaten by a predator, such as a fox.

Yes, when you're a lamb, you'd better learn to get up on your four knobbly legs if you don't want to end up as a fox's starter, main course and pudding.

Question: How come human babies don't get eaten by predators?

There's another strange and curious question.

Baby humans are taken care of and kept safe by their parents and, if not their parents, some pretty important grown-ups.

Humans *work together* to raise children. We build homes and gather food. We organize nurseries and schools and hospitals. We are a successful animal because we work together.

Team human!

Adults spend years and years and years and years and years and years and years caring for their children. Children grow and develop until they are around 25 years old.

When they are grown up, humans are capable of doing incredible things like landing a vehicle on Mars that sends pictures back to Earth. You can't really say that about a sheep.

They're cute and everything, but they're not great at inventions.

Baby Brains

Humans are born with brains, of course, but the brains we are born with are a long way from being finished. They've got a lot more growing to do. That's putting it mildly.

A baby brain is a bit like a bag of loose LEGO® bricks. They have a lot of potential, but not much is joined together. Unlike LEGO® kits, they don't even come with instructions.

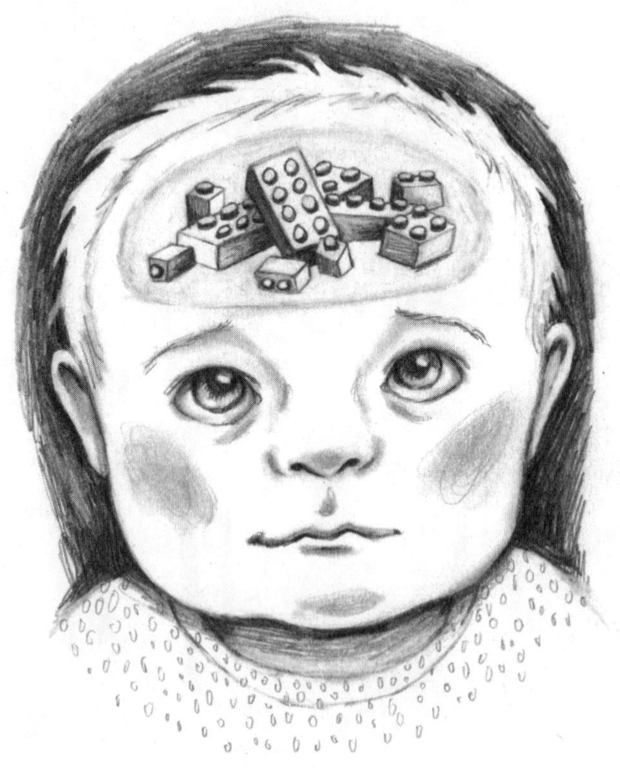

If they did come with instructions, baby brains wouldn't know how to read them. They don't know about words, pictures or paper. They don't even know they are separate little alive people. Babies really do have a lot to learn. They have to start from the very beginning, with a lot of help from their parents. They are completely reliant on those guys.

The building blocks in our baby brains join together and help us learn stuff when we have EXPERIENCES. That means we LEARN about the world we live in and experience.

When a baby or a young child experiences a world that is safe, comfortable and caring, that's what it learns. It learns that the world is safe, comfortable and caring.

It learns that adults look after you and make you laugh and give you food when you are hungry and help you go to sleep when you are tired. Their brains build lovely, safe models out of the loose building bricks.

When babies' brains think of adults, they think of nice smiles and trusting and feeling safe. When babies feel safe, they learn quickly and begin to explore their world.

When a baby or young child learns that its world is dangerous, it learns how to live in that dangerous world. This is about STAYING ALIVE, which is also known as SURVIVAL.

11

Baboon Alarm Time

Since Baboon Tuesday, I only have to hear the word 'baboon' and my heart races, my hands sweat, my jaw tightens and Amy Amygdala goes on to HIGH ALERT. In short, I am well stressed out.

My brain and my body have learnt from experience that baboons are dangerous.

KEEP AWAY FROM BABOONS, they warn me.

BABOON = BEWARE.

BE VERY WARE.

DANGER. DANGER.

TEETH.

EAT.

ME.

RUUUNNNNNN!

To keep me warned about baboons, my brain and my body have made a BABOON ALARM system. If I am reminded of baboons, my BABOON ALARM goes off.

When it goes off, I get panicky and I can't

concentrate. It doesn't take much to set off my BABOON ALARM.

If I walk past some random person and they are wearing the same body spray as the baboon was and that smell goes up my nose, it's BABOON ALARM TIME.

REMEMBERING BOX

Remember Amy, the nut-shaped piece of kit deep inside our brains? She scans for danger like a lifeguard at a swimming pool.

Baby brains have an Amy Amygdala, too.

If a baby's Amy Amygdala detects danger, she does all the things that mine did when the baboon scared me.

She makes the baby's heart beat fast, and she calls on Adrian Adrenaline and Courtney Cortisol to race around the baby's body, getting it ready to RUN from the danger, FIGHT the danger or HIDE from the danger.

Hang on a minute.

Can you guess what the problem is?

REMEMBERING BOX

Remember the difference between lambs and human babies?

Human babies can't run, can't fight and can't

even hide that well either. This makes them vulnerable to DANGER. This means it is important that babies have adults around them who protect them from danger and take really good care of them.

What babies can do really, really well is make an extremely loud noise. If there was a 'Who is the best at loudness?' competition, human babies would beat baby lambs hands- and trotters-down.

A baby's cry is almost impossible to ignore. It's designed that way. It's what helps to keep the baby safe.

Amy grabs the baby's controls and makes them SCREAM FOR THEIR LIFE. That scream gets the sudden attention of adults. The adults use their extra energy and focus to get the baby out of danger. PHEW!

The adults comfort and soothe the screaming baby. Soothing the baby allows its Amy Amygdala to calm down. It means Adrian Adrenaline and Courtney Cortisol take a break, and the baby can feel safe and calm again.

But what if the baby often feels scared by lots of shouting and loud noises?

What if the baby often feels hungry and doesn't get fed?

What if the baby is alone and doesn't get calmed by an adult when it cries?

The baby's brain learns that its world is unsafe. The models it builds out of the building bricks are about dangers, not safety. It builds a lot of ALARMS.

The baby will feel scared and stressed much of the time. Stress is not good for growing bodies and brains.

The baby will have a lot of ALARMS.

As the baby grows up, their alarms may get set off by words or memories. They may even be set off by a smell or a sound. When an alarm gets set off, the baby's body goes into PANIC STATIONS.

Children who have experienced trauma and learnt that the world is scary may FIGHT, RUN or HIDE a lot. It's not their fault. It is their body insisting 'I WILL SURVIVE'. It's automatic.

Here is what fighting, running or hiding might look like for a child who has experienced trauma:

- being aggressive
- having a hot temper
- moving around a lot
- finding it difficult to concentrate
- not being able to do silence
- not being able to do what someone else tells you to do
- gathering lots of things
- finding it hard to get organized
- telling fibs even when there's no need
- not trusting people
- feeling rubbish
- being very quiet
- not wanting to be noticed
- feeling pressure to keep everyone happy
- doing what you're told even if it harms you
- finding it hard to remember things
- finding it difficult to sleep
- not knowing when you are hot or cold, hungry, or in need of a wee or poo
- not feeling quite at home in your body
- finding it difficult to share
- difficulty keeping friends

Crumbs, that was a tricky list. Well done if you got to the end of it.

Sometimes this fighting, running or hiding gets confused with what ***Some People*** call 'bad behaviour'.

It's not bad behaviour. It's a sure sign a person doesn't feel safe. Yet.

Luckily for us humans, there are loads and loads of things that can help with our fighting, running and hiding, which we will get to very soon.

Luckily for humans, our brains grow and learn new things even when we are adults.

A Fact of Science and Kindness

We learn about the world we are born into. We learn about how safe it is.

We don't learn about the world someone else is born into.

It's why a person shouldn't ever say, 'I feel safe

and so should you.' Other people can't tell us a situation is safe when our bodies and brains have learnt it is not.

It is kinder, as well as better science, to ask, 'I wonder what happened to you that makes you feel unsafe. Let's work this out together.'

12

RRREWIND! A Bit of Remembering

If you've got this far, you already know loads and loads about brains and science and surviving. This is new and incredible science. You've already got a lot of superpower.

Next time you see a person get into a fright, you can say to them afterwards, 'There's this nut-shaped thing deep inside your brain called Amy Amygdala. Her job is to spot danger. Guess what? She just jumped into action.' That person will be extremely impressed.

You could explain to them, 'Two stress chemicals called Courtney Cortisol and Adrian Adrenaline rushed around your body getting you ready to fight, run or hide to keep you safe.'

Be sure to wait until that person is calm before you deliver your lesson because...well...can you remember why?

A brain that is busy fighting, running or hiding is not able to learn new things or hold a clever conversation. It just isn't.

Now give yourself a giant pat on the back.

13

Some People and Three Things They Say that Are WRONG

Some People

Some People are people who don't have the knowledge about trauma and are behind with the science. They have some catching up to do.

> ***WRONG THING #1***
> *When all the scary dangers have gone away, a person's body will know it is safe and go back to 'normal'.**

Some People think that when all the dangers have gone, Amy Amygdala, Adrian Adrenaline

*e.g. sit still, stop fidgeting, calm down, trust people.

and Courtney Cortisol will give up and go on a relaxing beach holiday. This is WRONG.

The fact is, bodies and brains that have lived in dangerous times have to learn how to feel safe. Even then, they're going to take a lot of convincing that they are safe. Years and years of convincing. Of course they are.

As we learnt right at the start, all living things have one NUMBER 1 aim: STAYING ALIVE.

STAYING ALIVE is pretty important.

All together now, STAYIN' ALIVE, STAYIN' ALIVE.

WRONG THING #2
It doesn't matter if your scary trauma happened when you were very young because you won't remember it.

This isn't true. In fact, it is very not true. It is WRONG.

As we know, trauma isn't just about remembering. We're talking much deeper inside the brain than that. We're talking deep inside where the sun don't shine. We're talking about the models our brains make to help us survive the world we are born into.

We're talking bodies, too.

Racing hearts, wide-open eyes and bees buzzing inside our tummies are our bodies remembering. We don't suddenly think to ourselves, 'I must remember to get my heart racing.' That would be ridiculous. These things happen automatically.

WRONG THING #3
That thing that happened to you was ages ago. You should be over it by now.

Some People believe that we get over scary

traumas like we recover from a runny nose or a gurgly tummy. Oh dear. WRONG.

If our bodies have learnt to survive dangerous times, that's their superpower. If we now live in a safer world, it's going to take a lot of getting used to. It's going to take a lot of kindness and understanding just for starters.

If I just 'got over' Baboon Tuesday, the following day I might stand under exactly the same tree, lick exactly the same type of lolly and get exactly the same kind of scare. And on Baboon Wednesday I might not be so lucky.

I might even find myself as pizza topping of the week at The Big Baboon Café and Disco. Which, I think we can agree, would not be good for my survival.

The trouble with Wrong Thing #1, Wrong Thing #2, Wrong Thing #3 and all the other Wrong Things is they are a bit judgey. Being judged by judgeyness can make a person feel ashamed that they are not somehow stronger.

'Why haven't I got over it yet?' they may ask themselves. 'Perhaps there is something wrong with me. Perhaps it was my fault. Why didn't I fight more, or run away faster or tell someone?' This can make a person feel **shame**.

Shame is strange and curious, but it is also a powerful and horrible feeling. It can make a person feel really bad. It can even make a person believe *they are bad*.

I hope you know why we don't just 'get over' trauma and why it's nothing like, say, getting over a runny nose or a gurgly tummy.

This is a good time for some more remembering.

REMEMBERING BOX

★ It is not a person's fault if they have experienced trauma.

★ It is not a person's fault if it is difficult for them to recover from trauma.

★ It is not a person's fault if they have ways of coping with trauma.

★ Coping with trauma is a strength and a superpower.

14

How to Grow Your Superpowers

Question: Is there a cure for trauma?

In a word, no. There is no 'cure' for trauma. There isn't a pill or a potion or a magic plaster or an operation that will remove it.

But there are lots of things that can really help. Really, really, really, really help.

Some people who have experienced trauma find that using their bodies helps them to feel more comfortable in the world. Running, bouncing, bending, cycling, disco dancing and drumming are all ways of getting to know our bodies better.

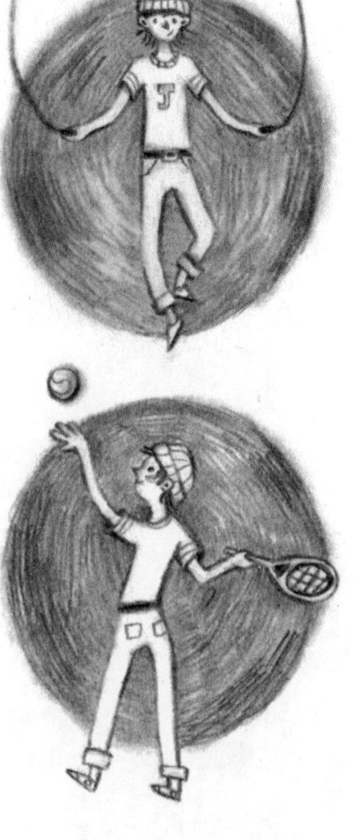

Work that body.

Sometimes we might be so busy with all the STAYING ALIVE business that we don't have the headspace to listen to what our body parts are telling us. Learning to listen to our bodies when they tell us they are hungry, cold, tired or in need of a giant wee or a poo is also bodywork and a top life skill. Like all top life skills, it takes practice.

When we get good at this trauma business, we can learn about our limits and find our power. We get to know where our ALARMS are.

We get to know when to say 'no' to something that we can't cope with and when we feel safe enough to say 'yes'. This is easier when we have people around us who take care of us and who understand trauma.

Being able to trust other people can take a long time.

If we can talk to people we trust and feel safe with, we can begin to make sense of our past and our present. We may even be able to think about our future.

It may feel strange to talk at first, and Amy Amygdala might reach for the driving controls and go on HIGH ALERT, but that's only her doing her job. She's learning what safety feels like.

Why Knowing about Trauma Is a Superpower

Knowing all about survival and trauma means we can understand and take care of ourselves and other people better. It can help us understand that experiencing trauma is not our fault and doesn't make us bad or weak.

It can help us understand that coping through scary times means a person is strong.

Knowing about trauma helps us to be aware of how our bodies feel. It can help us learn about what makes us feel calm and happy, and what stresses us right out.

Knowing how strange and curious trauma is gives us the words to explain it to other people. If we have experienced trauma, it gives us the choice to share with people we trust, 'I experienced trauma.' We might choose to share with them certain things we find difficult or scary. We might feel safe enough to let them help us.

Knowing about trauma is a superpower, and being kind is also a superpower.

If we know someone who has experienced trauma, we can imagine what their world might look and feel like to them. It might look and feel very different to the way our world looks and feels to us. This gives us the choice to notice when they might need some help to feel safer. This is kindness.

When we feel safe, us humans can go out into the world, make friends, learn stuff, have new experiences and achieve happy and satisfying lives. If we can help each other to achieve these things, it makes all of our lives better.

We don't often think of knowledge and kindness as superpowers, but they are. When they join together, knowledge and kindness are a super-duper power that can change lives and make the world a better place.

15

Baboon Tuesday 4: The Final Chapter

My name is Ordinary Jo. I will never forget Baboon Tuesday.

I will never forget what happened as I swung from the swing that dangles from The Big Tree on top of The Big Hill.

I will never forget that, thanks to my strange and curious body, I did not end up on the menu at The Big Baboon Café and Disco. I am very glad about that.

I enjoy my ordinary life.

I enjoy Bin Lorry Day. I enjoy saying 'morning' to Barry, Morris and Robyn, and I enjoy watching the bins being swung high, high into the sky.

I am looking forward to doing lots more ordinary things in my ordinary life. And maybe a few extra-ordinary things as well.

I have included Ordinary Jo's Main Learnings about Trauma at the back of this book.

This book is for you. Thank you for reading it or listening to it or reading it aloud to someone you care about. You're helping to spread the knowledge and to spread the kindness.

Hooray for knowledge and kindness. And hooray for you.

Dear Ordinary Jo,

My buddy Barry the Bin Lorry Driver told me I frightened you when I dropped out of the tree that day. I'm sorry, man!

I didn't mean to scare you.

Dude, I love that film, the one with the dumb goats. I just wanted to watch it.

But you looked like you'd seen a ghost and threw your lolly in the dirt! I can't resist a lolly, especially an orange one. And before I had time to ask you for a lick, you took off like your poor ordinary butt was on fire!

Look, man, my name's Tony. I own The Big Baboon – the café and disco in town. As a way of saying sorry, come by sometime and choose whatever you like from the menu. You might wanna come on a Saturday night. Saturday nights are disco night. They're wild! I could show you some moves... Let's be friends, dude!

Oh, and I got your phone.

Big baboon hugs,

Tony

P.S. Promise I won't eat you!

Ordinary Jo's Main Learnings about Trauma

- Our bodies are very concerned with Stayin' Alive.
- Our bodies are on the lookout for possible dangers, every second of every day, even while we're getting on with other stuff.
- When our bodies spot a danger, they protect us by fighting the danger off, running from it or hiding from it.
- Baby humans rely on their adults to do a lot of the fighting, running and hiding for them. They call their adults with the use of LOUD CRYING and SCREAMING.
- Babies learn about how safe or unsafe their world is and how to survive in that world.
- Carrots grow around stones and other obstacles. This is carrot survival.
- When humans experience a big threat to their safeness, it is called trauma.
- Trauma is like an invisible, inside hurt.

- ★ It is not a person's fault if they have experienced trauma.
- ★ Living with trauma is being strong.
- ★ ***Some People*** confuse fighting, running and hiding with 'bad behaviour' and don't yet know enough about bravery and strength.
- ★ Sheep are not great at science, but they are good at staying alive and safe from foxes.
- ★ It takes time and good relationships and growing to learn how to feel safe.
- ★ We can all learn new things even when we are adults, and especially when we feel safe and cared for.

Tony is teaching Ordinary Jo to disco dance. Jo's favourite song to dance to is called Stayin' Alive.

also by Sally Donovan

Billy Bramble and The Great Big Cook Off

A Story about Overcoming Big, Angry Feelings at Home and at School

Illustrated by Kara McHale

'Want to know something else about me? I am Billy Bramble: the King, the President and the Emperor of Bad Lucksville. I am the Chief Executive of Bad Luck Limited, the Bad Luck Champion of the World, the Bad Luck Guinness World Record holder and it's all thanks to my invisible dog Gobber. He's my Bringer of Bad Luck.'

Billy Bramble likes rude words, smelly farts, loud farts and freestyle sneezing but when BAD THINGS happen, his invisible angry dog Gobber barks in his ears, gives him brain mash and breaks things. One day a competition is announced at school – The Great Big Cook Off – can Billy Bramble defeat Gobber and change his epic bad luck?

An irreverent story for children aged 8–12 about a less than perfect boy, this book will inspire any child who's ever secretly thought they might be less than perfect too.

£8.99 | $13.95 | PB | 192PP | ISBN 978 1 84905 663 2 | EISBN 978 1 78450 164 8

of related interest

Outsmarting Worry

An Older Kid's Guide to Managing Anxiety

Dawn Huebner PhD
Illustrated by Kara McHale

Worry has a way of growing, shifting from not-a-big-deal to a VERY BIG DEAL in the blink of an eye. This big-deal Worry is tricky, luring children into behaviours that keep the anxiety cycle going. Children often find it hard to fight back against Worry, but not anymore. *Outsmarting Worry* teaches 9–13-year-olds and the adults who care about them a specific set of skills that makes it easier to face – and overcome – worries and fears. Smart, practical, proven techniques are presented in language immediately accessible to children with an emphasis on shifting from knowing to doing, from worried to happy and free.

Dawn Huebner, PhD is a Clinical Psychologist specializing in the treatment of anxious children and their parents. She is the author of the award-winning *What to Do When Your Worry Too Much* and five other *What to Do Guides for Kids*. She lives in Exeter, New Hampshire.

£9.99 | $15.95 | PB | 112PP | ISBN 978 1 78592 782 9 | EISBN 978 1 78450 702 2

Sibling Survival Guide

Surefire Ways to Solve Conflicts, Reduce Rivalry, and Have More Fun with your Brothers and Sisters

Dawn Huebner

Illustrated by Kara McHale

Having a brother or sister can be tough. It can also be great, but it's hard to see the great parts with so many bad parts getting in the way. Problems like fighting and bossing. Teasing and jealousy. Tattling. Pestering. And more.

But what if you could do something about those problems? Clear them away? Then you'd be able to actually enjoy your siblings!

This indispensable guide from best-selling author Dr. Dawn Huebner speaks directly to children ages 9–12, teaching skills to help them manage feelings and resolve conflicts, strengthening the bonds between brothers and sisters.

Warm, witty, and packed with practical strategies, this interactive book is the complete resource for educating, motivating, and empowering siblings to live in peace.

£12.99 | $17.95 | PB | 128PP | ISBN 978 1 78775 491 1 | EISBN 978 1 78775 492 8

Doodle Your Worries Away

A CBT Doodling Workbook for Children Who Feel Worried or Anxious

Tanja Sharpe

Foreword by Suzanne Alderson

This workbook draws on CBT and creative therapy methods to help children aged 8+ understand their worry and anxiety.

Featuring 50 fun and engaging doodling activities, this book allows young people to tune into their worries and their sources, using creativity to process anxiety, and building confidence to find their own solutions. This exploration can be independently led by the child themselves or with guidance from a parent or professional.

Drawn from over 15 years of experience of supporting young people with anxiety, this workbook takes an integrative approach and is a valuable resource for anyone looking to support a child experiencing worry.

Tanja Sharpe is an integrative counsellor, therapeutic coach and creative therapist, specialising in CBT and mindfulness. She leads creative therapy workshops and training courses and is the founder of both Creative Counsellors and Confident Hearts. She is based in Chester, UK.

£12.99 | $19.95 | PB | 128PP | ISBN 978 1 78775 790 5 | EISBN 978 1 78775 791 2

The Can-Do Kid's Journal

Discover Your Confidence Superpower!

Sue Atkins

Illustrated by Amy Bradley

This journal will help kids feel more confident, relaxed and happy in all aspects of their life. Adorned with fun illustrations, it is designed to develop a can-do attitude that encourages 'having a go', accepting that mistakes might be made along the way. From this, kids can develop the mindset to take the small steps needed to make big dreams come true.

Full of practical techniques and fun activities, from drawing and colouring, to thought-provoking questions, this journal from parenting expert Sue Atkins will empower children to build resilience and a growth mindset. It is the perfect tool to help kids find their superpowers and put small changes into practice that will make a big difference to their lives.

Sue Atkins spent 25 years as a teacher and Deputy Head, before becoming a parenting coach 10 years ago. She is well-known as 'The Parenting Expert' and frequently appears across the media, including on TV such as ITV's This Morning, Sky News and in many of the UK's biggest newspapers. www.sueatkinsparentingcoach.com

Amy Bradley has previously illustrated books such as *The Art of Being a Brilliant Teenager* and *Diary of a Brilliant Kid*. She is based in Staffordshire. www.amybradley.co.uk

£14.99 | $19.95 | PB | 144PP | ISBN 978 1 78775 271 9

Help! My Feelings Are Too Big!

Making Sense of Yourself and the World After a Difficult Start in Life – for Children with Attachment Issues

K. L. Aspden
Foreword by Louise Michelle Bombèr
Illustrated by Charlotte Portier-Tock

Emotions can be complicated at the best of times. If something goes wrong right at the beginning of someone's life things can often feel painful and confusing.

This book will help explain that there are always good reasons why a person feels the way they do. It will help you learn about emotions like anxiety, how you can live with these emotions, and how safe adults can help you build a calm, strong place inside yourself!

Designed to help build emotional awareness, this book offers friendly support for children aged 9–12 who have attachment disorders, anxiety or are overcoming early trauma and is an invaluable tool for anyone supporting children with extreme emotions or attachment issues, including parents and carers, support workers, teachers, and therapists.

K. L. Aspden has worked as a therapist with both children and adults since 1998. She has particular interest in the areas of trauma and anxiety, and she has experience working in both mainstream and special schools. K. L. Aspden currently works in private practice with children with emotional and behavioural difficulty. She lives in East Sussex, UK.

£9.99 | $13.95 | PB | 64PP | ISBN 978 1 78592 556 6 | EISBN 978 1 78450 951 4